READING FOR LEARNING

Level Two

A book about

WORKING

Contents

HELEN ARNOLD

First published 1990

Published by
MACMILLAN EDUCATION LTD
Houndmills, Basingstoke, Hampshire RG21 2XS
and London
Companies and representatives
throughout the world

Printed in Hong Kong

ISBN 0-333-48006-6

Acknowledgements
The publishers would like to thank the following for their help in the research and development of this book: Bob Arthur, Bob Douglas, Sallie Purkis, Jenny Vaughan, Linda Taylor.

Illustrations: Maggie Brand (Maggie Mundy).

Design: Amanda Chant
Typeset by Quadraset Ltd, Midsomer Norton, Avon
Produced for Macmillan Education by Tim and Jenny Wood Editorial Consultants.

The author and publishers would like to thank the following for their kind permission to reproduce copyright material: 'Inuit woman's work song' from *Eskimo poems from Canada and Greenland* translated by Tom Lowenstein and published by Allison and Busby; 'Hunting song' ('Hunting song — the deer speaks') and 'Call to sing while liquor ferments ('A rain-making song') Ruth M Underhill, *Papago Indian religion* Copyright © 1946, 1973 Columbia University Press. Used by permission; 'The herd-boy' translated from the Chinese by Arthur Waley in *170 Chinese poems*; 'A Sioux warrior's song to his horse' from *American Indians sing* by Charles Hoffman. (Thomas Y. Crowell) Copyright © 1967 by Charles Hoffman; 'The ballad of the big hewer' words and music by Ewen McColl and Peggy Seeger. Used by permission of Harmony Music; 'Pick a bale o' cotton' H Ledbetter, A Lomax and J Lomax © 1962 Kensington Music Ltd, 19/20 Poland Street, London W1V 3DD. International Copyright Secured. All Rights Reserved. Used by Permission. English version of Maori chant, 'Chant before battle', arranged by Allen Curnow and Roger Oppenheim from *The Penguin book of New Zealand verse* edited by Allen Curnow, 1960 published by Penguin; 'The Old Chisholm trail' A Lomax and J Lomax © 1966 TRO Essex Music Ltd, 19/20 Poland Street, London W1V 3DD. International Copyright Secured. All Rights Reserved. Used by Permission; 'The Inuit dance song' from *Primitive song* by C M Bowra published by Weidenfeld and Nicolson Ltd.

Every effort has been made to trace copyright holders, but if any omissions have been made please let us know.

Introduction

What is work?

'Work' is a funny word. It can mean so many different things. It can mean cleaning the house and cooking the supper. It can mean digging the garden or mending things.

It can also mean doing something to earn money. People do this in all sorts of different ways. You can probably think of many of them. Some people work in shops or offices and others work in factories. Some people work out of doors, mending the roads or in parks and gardens. Farmers work by keeping animals and growing food for the rest of us to eat. Some people work in noisy factories. Some work by the sea and others work in mines, deep under the ground.

The first part of this book is about people working many years ago, before there were towns or shops or factories.

The second part of the book is about people working in Britain, about the time when your great great grandparents lived.

Their stories are told through the songs that people sang about their work.

Inuit

North America

Sioux

Britain

Europe

Papago

Afric

South America

This map shows where the people you can read about in this book lived and worked.

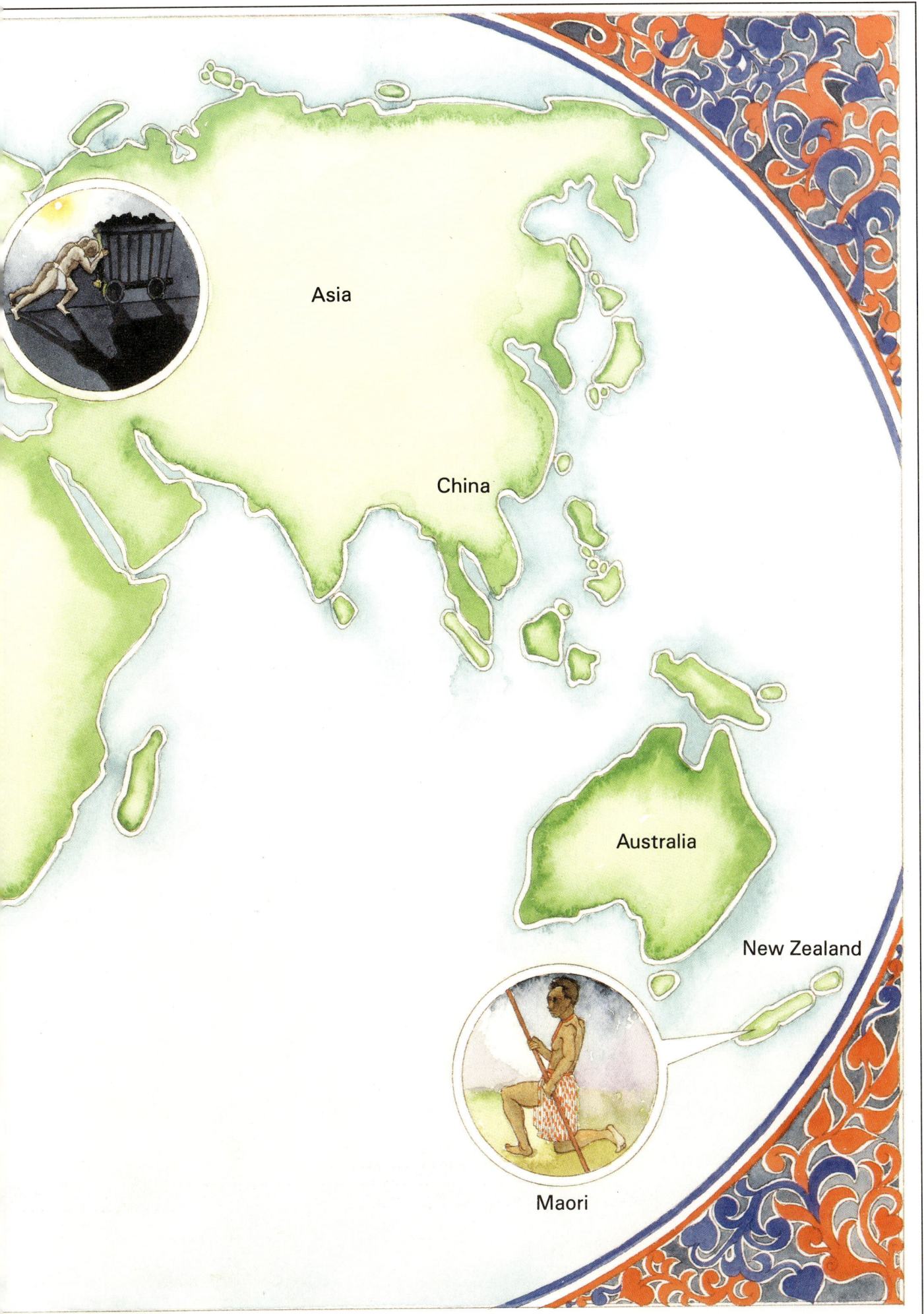

Asia

China

Australia

New Zealand

Maori

1   The people of the far north

Long ago, there were no towns and cities, roads, railways or electricity. Life was hard. People lived in small groups of a few families. They had to find ways of getting food. Many of them **hunted** for it.

The **Inuit** people live in the far north of Canada and Alaska. They also live in Greenland. People used to call the Inuit people Eskimos.

In the past, they lived mainly by hunting. The men went out to catch fish, seals, bears, birds and walruses.

Seal hunting song

Seal, seal
I know you swim
warm and safe
in this ice-covered sea.
Think of me, seal,
think of me,
this little man
sitting cold and alone
in his hunting hut.

Think of me, seal,
and come.
I call to you,
I call to you!
Hear me, hear me,
Warm seal in the
winter sea.

In the places where the Inuit live it is freezing cold for nine months of the year.

In the past, the only way Inuit hunters could travel across the snow was by walking, or using sledges. They made shelters for themselves, from blocks of snow.

In summer, they often lived in tents made from animal skin. They worked hard all summer, drying food so that it would keep through the winter. They also found time to make beautiful carved tools and ornaments.

♪ **An Inuit woman's work song**
*I'm a little woman
who's happy to work,
happy to toil.
Anxious to be useful,
I pick willow flowers
that remind me of
the grey wolf's beard.*

*I wear holes in my mocassins
when I walk far out
to pluck the willow flowers
that remind me of
the grey wolf's beard
the grey wolf's beard.*

The Inuit men looked brave as they set out across the snow. But they did not always feel brave inside themselves. So they made up songs to make themselves feel better.

On the next page is an Inuit dance song. The men danced, and as they danced, they sang. They were thinking about hunting, even when they were dancing.

Inuit dance song

How am I to strike this one with a missile?
As it walks, let me strike it.
Since I cannot do it with a winged arrow.
With a stone let me strike it.

How am I to strike this one?
The king-eider — let me strike it.
Since I cannot do it with a winged arrow
With a stone let me strike it.

How am I to strike this one?
The hare here — let me strike it.
Since I cannot do it with a winged arrow,
With a snare let me attack it.

How am I to strike this one?
The black musk-ox — let me strike it.
Since I cannot do it with a winged arrow,
with the horn of my bow let me push it away.

2 Fighters, hunters and farmers

The **Papago** people are Native Americans. Native Americans are also sometimes called North American Indians. There are many groups of Native Americans. The Papago come from Arizona, in the south-west of the United States. You can see where they come from if you look at the map on pages 4 and 5.

The Papago were farmers. Sometimes they went hunting. This is a song they sang about hunting deer. It is supposed to be a deer talking. They felt sorry for the deer.

Hunting song

Here I come forth.
On the earth, I fell over.
The snapping bow made me dizzy.

Here I come forth!
On the mountain I slipped;
The humming arrow made me dizzy.

The fence of bows!
Within it I run about
In every direction, looking.

The fence of arrows!
Within it I run about
In every direction, looking.

Already they have killed me.
This is my flesh they cut.
And here they threw it down.

The people who lived long ago had to protect their homes from enemies. Another group of people might fancy their land and crops, or their horses or their cattle!

There are many battle songs and chants. The fighting men, called warriors, sang their own battle chant to make themselves feel strong. They wanted to feel strong enough to win the fight.

This song comes from New Zealand. It was sung by the **Maori** people, who used to be the only people living there.

♪ ***Chant before battle***
Let fog fill the skies.
Let the cloud cover them,
the wind howls high up
to the world away down.
Listen! The wind howls
from far away down!

Shuddering, the spear
is charging, is flying,
the twin-bladed shark,
and the footsteps hurtling.
O furious the footsteps,
blood-wet the footsteps
bound for the world's brink.

He goes, god of battles,
the stars in his stride
and the moon in his stride —
run, run from the death-blow! ♪

11

Horses were useful for hunting and fighting. The **Sioux** people are another group of Native Americans. They used to hunt on horseback.

They loved their horses. They worked hard looking after them and prayed that they would be strong and quick.

A Sioux warrior's song to his horse
My horse be swift in flight,
Even like a bird.
My horse be swift in flight.
Bear me now in safety.
Far from the enemy's arrows,
And you shall be rewarded
With streamers and ribbons red.
My horse be swift in flight.

The hunters and farmers of long ago
had to work hard.

Children often looked after animals
such as sheep, cows and goats. They
did not go to school.

This is a song from China. It is about
800 years old and it is about a herd
boy.

♪ *In the southern village, the boy who minds the ox*
With his naked feet stands on the ox's back.
Through the hole in his coat the river wind blows;
Through his broken hat the mountain rain pours.
On the long dyke he seemed to be far away;
In the narrow lane suddenly we were face to face.
The boy is home and the ox is back in the stall;
And a dark smoke oozes through the thatched roof. ♫

The people of long ago were often farmers who grew crops to eat.

It was harder to grow crops in those days. The people had to make their own tools. They had no tractors or other farm machines. They did not have modern ways of watering the land by pumping it from lakes and rivers. They did not have modern weedkillers and fertilisers.

Sometimes something went wrong with the crops. Perhaps they were attacked by pests, or washed away in a flood. Often, crops died because there was not enough rain. All these things can still happen to farmers all over the world.

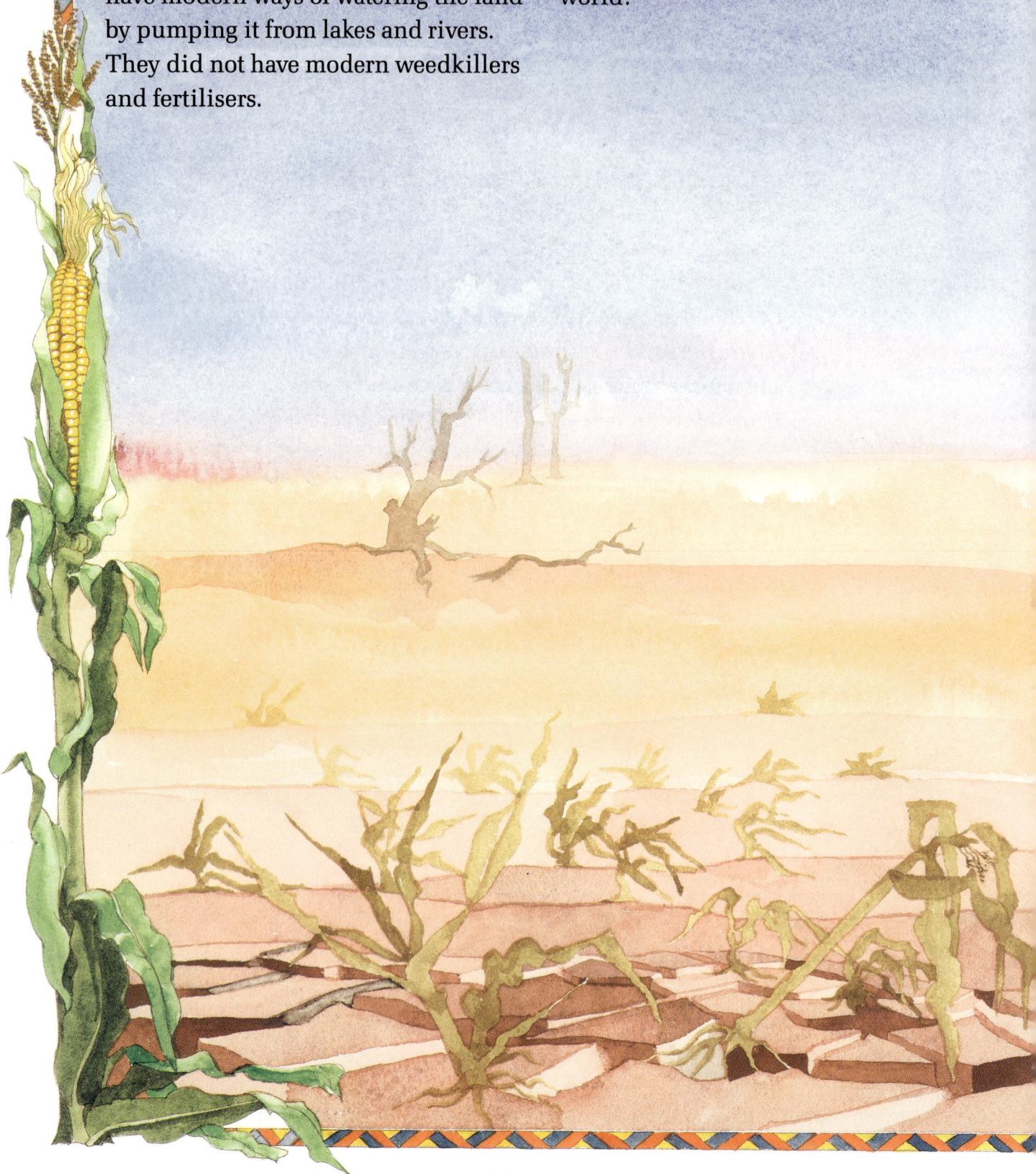

Many groups of people had Rainmakers. Their job was to pray for rain. Here is a Rainmaker's song that was sung by Native Americans. It tells about working on the land as well.

A rain-making song

Come together!
You shall see this thing which we have always done
And what must truly happen.
Because we have planned it thus and thus have done.
Right soon, indeed, it will happen.
It will rain.
The fields will be watered.
Therein we shall drop the seed.
Seed which bears corn of all colours;
Seed which grows big.
Thus we shall do.
Thereby we shall feed ourselves;
Thereby our stomachs shall grow big;
Thereby we shall live.

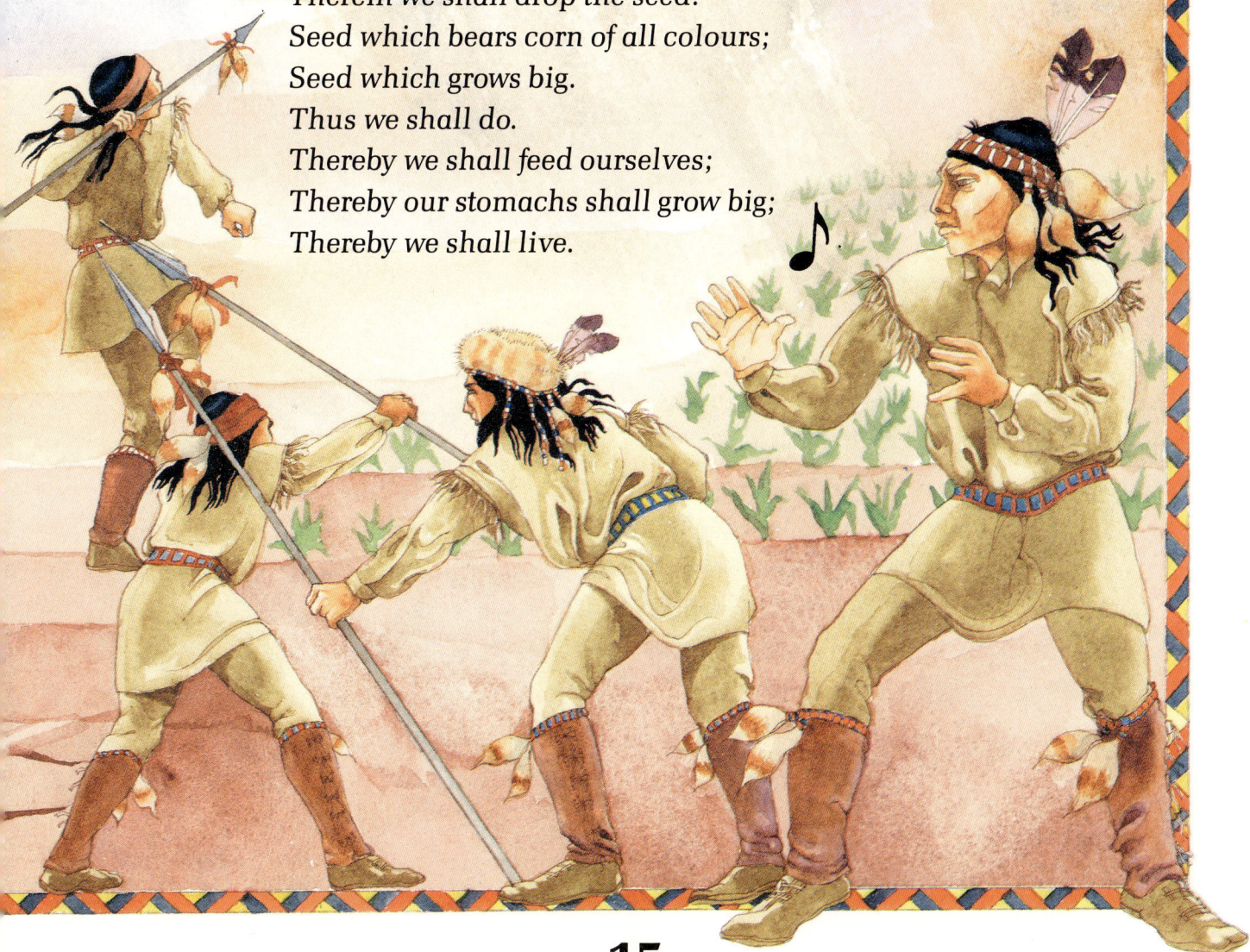

3　Cowboys and slaves

For thousands of years, the people of North America had their land to themselves. The Inuit hunted and fished. The Papago and people like them farmed their land. The Sioux roamed over the grassy plains.

But then, about 400 years ago, people started to come from Europe to settle in North America. They farmed the land where the Native Americans used to live. They put herds of cattle on the grasslands, where the Sioux once lived and hunted.

The herds of cattle were large. Cowboys rode with them, keeping them safe, rounding them up and driving the herds to market. These cowboys sang as they kept the cattle moving in the daytime. At night, they sang to keep the cattle quiet.

This is a song from about 100 years ago. It is about the old Chisholm Trail. This ran for 1600 miles, from Texas in the south to Wyoming in the north. It wasn't really a road — it was just the way cowboys drove the cattle.

There are a few unusual words in this song. **Prairie** is a word for the grassy plains in the centre of North America. You can see them on a map of the United States and Canada. **Longhorns** are a kind of cattle. **Sonsagun** is just a name the cowboy calls the cattle.

The old Chisholm Trail

1 Come along, boys, and listen to my tale,
   I'll tell you of my troubles on the old Chisholm Trail.
   Chorus:
   Come-a-ky-yi-yippy, come-a-ky-yi-yea,
   Come-a-ky-yi-yippy, come-a-ky-yi-yea.

2 A ten-dollar horse and a forty-dollar saddle,
   And I'm going punching Texas cattle.
   (Chorus)

3 It's bacon and beans most every day,
   I'd sooner be eating prairie hay.
   (Chorus)

4 It's raining and hailing and blowing mighty cold,
   And these longhorn sonsaguns are getting hard to hold.
   (Chorus)

5 My feet in the stirrups, my seat in the sky,
   Gonna quit herding cows in the sweet bye and bye.
   (Chorus)

6 I'm going to town to spend my money.
   Then I'm going back South to see my honey.
   (Chorus)

People from Europe were not the only newcomers to North America. There were also many Africans.

The Africans did not choose to travel to North America. They had been captured in Africa and brought across the sea in ships. They were sold as slaves to work on big farms called plantations. There were slaves in North America and in the Caribbean islands.

Slaves are made to work without pay. They were often treated cruelly.

In North America, many slaves had to work hard in the cotton fields. This is a song that they sometimes sang. The slaves sang as they worked to keep going, and to ask God to help them. Listen to the beat of this song. It made it easier to pick cotton all day in the hot sun.

Pick a bale o' cotton

1 Jump down, turn around,
   Pick a bale o' cotton,
   Jump down, turn around,
   Pick a bale a day.
   (Chorus)
   O-Lawdy,
   Pick a bale o' cotton.
   O-Lawdy,
   Pick a bale a day.

2 Old Massa give me one dram to
   Pick a bale o' cotton.
   Old Massa give me one dram to
   Pick a bale a day.
   (Chorus)

3 Me and my partner can
   Pick a bale o' cotton.
   Me and my partner can
   Pick a bale of hay.
   (Chorus)

4 Dirty jobs

This chapter is about life in Britain, about 150 years ago. Work then was different from today. It was much dirtier and people had fewer machines to help them. They had to work hard, by hand.

People built machines from iron and steel. They built roads and railways. They mined for coal. They built houses and factories.

Here is a song about building railway tracks.

1   All you that delight in the railway making,
    Come listen awhile to what I do sing;
    In summer time, they will use you all well,
    In winter you'd best stay at home with your girl.
    Chorus:
    That's the rule of the railway makers,
    Rare, good, jolly bankers, O

2   Now when we come to the bottom run,
    We fill our barrows right up to our chin.
    We fill our barrows, right up, breast high;
    And if you can't wheel it, another will try.
    (Chorus)

3   Our master comes with a staff in his hand:
    He knows very well how to measure the land.
    He measures our digging, so deep and so wide,
    He measures it well for his own side.

Bankers is another word for workers.

Long ago, men, women and even children worked in coal mines, far under the ground. This is a song about coal mining.

The ballad of the big hewer

1   Out of the dirt and darkness I was born —
    Go down.
    Out of the hard, black coalface I was torn —
    Go down.
    Kicked on the world and the earth split open.
    Crawled through a crack where the rock was broken.
    Burrowed a hole away in the coal —
    Go down.

2   Three hundred years I hewed at the coal by hand —
    Go down.
    In the pits of Durham and East Northumberland —
    Go down.
    Been gassed and burned and blown asunder.
    Buried more times than I can number.
    Getting the coal, away in the hole,
    Go down.

3   I've scrabbled and picked at the face where the roof was low
    Go down.
    Crawled in the seams where only a mole could go —
    Go down.
    In the thin cut seams I've ripped and redded,
    Where even the rats are born bow legged.
    Winning the coal away in the hole —
    Go down.

    (**Redded** means **cleared**.)

Working on the land was very hard work in those days. This is a song for a farmer's boy — a young boy who worked on a farm.

The rest of the day's own

One day when I was out of work, a job I went to seek,
To be a farmer's boy.
At last I found an easy job, at half a crown a week,
To be a farmer's boy.
The farmer said 'I think I've got the very job for you;
Your duties will be light, for this is all you've got to do:
Rise at three every morn, milk the cow with the crumpled horn,
Feed the pigs, clean the sty, teach the pigeons the way to fly,
Plough the fields, sow the hay, help the cocks and hens to lay,
Sow the seeds, tend the crops, chase the flies from the turnip tops,
Clean the knives, black the shoes, scrub the kitchen and sweep the flues,
Help the wife, wash the pots, grow the cabbages and carrots,
Make the beds, dust the coals, mend the gramophone,
And if there's no more work to do, the rest of the day's your own.'

(**Half a crown** was a coin worth 12½p — but you could buy a lot more with it in those days. **Flues** are chimneys.)

21

5 Cleaning jobs

In most houses, Monday was washing day. There were no washing machines or driers. It took all day to scrub the clothes, wring them, and hang them out.

Washing day

1 My Kate she is a bonny wife, there's none more free from evil.
Except upon a washing day, and then she is a devil.
The very kittens on the hearth, they dare not even play!
Away they jump, with many a thump, upon a washing day.
Chorus:
For it's thump, thump, scold, scold, thump, thump away;
The devil a bit of comfort's there upon a washing day.

2 The sky with clouds was overcast, the rain began to fall,
My wife she beat the children, and raised a pretty squall.
(Chorus)

Wash-day

They that wash on Monday,
Have all the week to dry;
They that wash on Tuesday,
They have pretty nigh;
They that wash on Wednesday,
Have half the week past;
They that wash on Thursday,
Are very near the last;
They that wash on Friday,
Wash for need;
They that wash on Saturday,
Are sluts indeed.

Nobody would ever dream of washing
on Sunday, or of doing any other work.
That was the holiday, when everyone
went to church.

Many of the songs in this part of the
book are unhappy ones. Perhaps they
helped people to keep going when the
work was very hard. If you enjoy
working, you may not need to cheer
yourself up by singing. But you can
still sing their songs and remember the
work they had to do.

23

Index